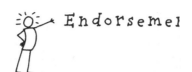 Endorsemel

MW01098458

"As a sketchnoter, I constantly hear teachers say they would love to try it with their classes but have no idea where to begin. Sylvia Duckworth has come to the rescue with this great primer to get you started. Filled with accessible activities for all ages, this book is perfect for everyone who sees the tremendous impact visual note-taking can have on retention, comprehension, and mental wellness. Thank you Sylvia, for giving us all the opportunity to colour outside the lines!"

—**Jen Giffen,** digital literacy resource teacher, York Region District School Board, Richmond Hill, Ontario, Canada, @VirtualGiff, VirtualGiff.com

"Those of us who love to sketchnote—and want to help others learn—ultimately hit a hurdle: The 'but I can't draw!' excuse. Sylvia's book helps alleviate the fear of drawing as she helps learners, step-by-step, to embrace their inner artists and create their own personal style. Everyone CAN draw, but sketchnoting is about much more than art. Breaking ideas into visuals tickles our brains and makes us productive and HAPPY. Thanks, Sylvia, for forging the way for another flood of sketchers who will soon believe in themselves and the power of sketching!"

—**Michele Osinski,** fifth-grade teacher, Temecula, California, @CheleOh, Techfairies.com

"I am blown away by Sylvia's comprehensive guide/ manual for sketchnoting for teachers and students. It contains a wealth of useful resources as well as ideas and activities to get started with this visual form of thinking, reflecting, and making your learning visible."

—**Silvia Tolisano,** author of *A Guide to Documenting Learning* and globally connected learning consultant, Florida, USA, @langwitches, langwitches.org/blog

"If you have heard about sketchnoting and are curious how to get started, you need this book! Sylvia gives you simple activities and ideas on how to brush up your doodling skills and the basics of visual note-taking (accompanied by her inspiring artwork). This book is definitely a go-to for anyone who's ready to try out sketchnotes!"

—**Misty Kluesner,** digital innovation, ToSA, Campbell Union School District, Felton, California, @MistyKluesner, bit.ly/MistyKluesner

"Sylvia creates low-stakes, simple entry points for any aspiring doodler to start creating and layering meaning with images, stylized fonts, and organization. I dream of all the students and educators who will read this book, practice, and eventually see themselves as artists. What a lifelong gift!"

—**Cate Tolnai,** director of member engagement, CUE, Sierra Madre, California, USA, @catetolnai, catetolnai.com

"Sylvia has created a great manual of the basics of how to sketchnote for yourself or have students use visual note-taking to support learning. In addition, she includes engaging activities and tips to teach students to become comfortable using sketchnoting to help them retain content and use 'both sides' of their brains!"

—**Kathy Schrock,** adjunct professor, higher ed graduate students, Wilkes University (PA), Eastham, Massachusetts, USA, @kathyschrock, kathyschrock.net

"As someone who has no background in sketchnoting, drawing, or visual arts of any kind, I finished this book feeling well-equipped and confident to try sketchnoting myself and with students. Not only does Sylvia share the benefits of this creative exercise (both academic and social/emotional), she also includes many practical activities and resources that teachers can use immediately with their classes."

—**Kim Pollishuke,** digital literacy resource teacher, York Region District School Board, Thornhill, Ontario, Canada, KimPollishuke.com, @KimPollishuke

"Are you ready to take the next step with sketchnotes in your classroom and beyond? Sylvia Duckworth's *How to Sketchnote: A Step-by-Step Manual for Teachers and Students* is a treasure chest of ideas! In this book, you have everything at your fingertips to get started on your sketchnote journey. From insights on why and how to support students with visual vocabularies and sketchnotes to super fun activities and drawing challenges, Sylvia shares everything you need to know, including the secret that everyone can draw! You don't have to be an artist to sketchnote, and everyone can benefit from doodling . . . so jump in and try it!"

—**Ann Kozma,** teacher innovation lead, Fullerton, California, USA, @annkozma723, techtravelteach.com

"Sylvia Duckworth's book is a straightforward, non-intimidating sketchnoting guide for beginners, full of beautiful and easy-to-recreate visuals. First-time sketchnoters of any age can get started immediately creating sketchnoting icons that will help them *draw* connections to information in unique and memorable ways. This book gives readers challenges to get their ideas flowing, provides a starting point from which to begin connecting with others in the community, and interweaves resources throughout the pages in ways that make this book come alive right before you. Use this book to lay the perfect foundation to launch your and your students' sketchnoting journey today!"

—**Valeria Rodriguez,** middle school science teacher, Miami, Florida, USA, @valeriasketches, valeriasketches.com

"If you are looking to incorporate sketchnoting in your classroom, this book is a must-have! Novice and experienced sketchnoters alike will grow from the activities provided. Best of all, the steps are easily applied to any age or subject."

—**Wanda Terral,** district technology coordinator, Lakeland, Tennessee, USA, @wterral, ignitionEDU.com

"Sylvia Duckworth is the queen of classroom sketchnoting. I remember after meeting her having my husband show me one of her graphics he had seen reshared on Facebook. That was when I realized not only how important sketchnotes are to the transmission of educational information but also how naturally awesome Sylvia is at mastering them. Sit down with this book to have your own personal mentor of sketchnoting and start empowering you and your students to supercharge ideas and learning."

—**Vicki Davis,** teacher and IT director, Camilla, Georgia, CoolCatTeacher.com, @coolcatteacher

"Sketchnoting is a fantastic instructional strategy to use with students to deepen learning, but many teachers are unsure where to start. Sylvia Duckworth has provided the answer to this question with her practical book *How to Sketchnote.* I particularly love how Sylvia has included so many helpful ways for learners of any age to expand and develop their 'personal library' of icons to use in sketchnotes. Whether you are a complete novice to sketchnoting or have been using it for many years with your students, Sylvia's book will provide you with ideas, strategies, and exercises that can help you become an even more skilled and savvy sketchnoting educator. Hooray for visual literacy, sketchnoting as a learning strategy, and Sylvia Duckworth for sharing this important contribution to our digital toolkits as technology using teachers!"

— **Dr. Wesley Fryer,** author of *Playing with Media: Simple Ideas for Powerful Sharing* and the ShowWithMedia.com media project framework, @wfryer

Sylvia Duckworth

How To
Sketchnote:
A Step-By-Step Manual
for TEACHERS
and STUDENTS

Visual Note-taking MADE EASY

Published by ElevateBooksEdu

©2015 Google Inc. All rights reserved. Google and the Google Logo are registered trademarks of Google Inc.

Library of Congress Control Number: 201895492
Paperback ISBN: 978-1-7336468-6-4
eBook ISBN: 978-1-7336468-7-1

Contents

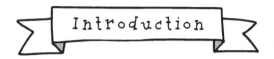

Introduction

"What do I need another social media platform for?" I asked my friend Joelle Rudick, who was trying to convince me to sign up for Twitter. "My life is busy enough!" But when she told me that many educators were already using Twitter as a great place to get inspiration and teaching ideas, I joined up. That was back in 2011. (To @joellerudick: Thank you for this life-changing tip!)

Fast-forward a couple of years. I started to notice some beautiful drawings in my Twitter feed related to education. People used the drawings to capture ideas from blog posts, articles, sermons, keynotes, and from their own thoughts in a very creative and visually appealing way. The hand-drawn images, filled with colour and detail, captivated me. *What is this wonderful thing, and how do I do it?* I wondered. I had to find out more.

I learned that these drawings were called Sketchnotes, and I reached out to my soon-to-be mentors Karen Bosch and Silvia Tolisano, whose stunning Sketchnotes appeared frequently in my Twitter feed. I found out that both of them draw on an iPad, and they recommended some apps and styluses. They also provided links to their wonderful sketchnoting resources, which I devoured (see index for resources).

To this day, Karen and Silvia, along with many other sketchnoting gurus like Mike Rohde, Sunni Brown, Doug Neill, and Diane Bleck, continue to inspire me. More recently, a number of "edusketchnoters" have become leaders in promoting sketchnoting amongst educators and students: Carrie Baughum, Royan Lee, Wanda Terrell, Cate Tolnai, Misty Kluesner, Ann Kozma, Nichole Carter, Jen Giffen, Marie-Andrée Ouimet, Beth Matusiewicz, Michele Osinski, and other educators are behind the fabulous #Sketch50 initiative (Sketch50.org). They have helped bring sketchnoting to the forefront of education (see index for their Twitter handles and resources), and teachers around the world are finally taking notice of this powerful tool for students to capture and display their learning.

3 rules for sketchnoting

1. Everyone can draw.

2. You will improve with practice.

3. It's about the ideas, not the art.

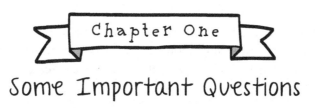

Some Important Questions

1. What is sketchnoting?

Sketchnoting is a form of visual note-taking, where you draw or doodle your thoughts, observations, or notes in combination with words or text. Sketchnoting is *not* art. It is a very personal way to document your thought process. The thing I emphasize over and over again to beginner sketchnoters is that **you do not have to be an artist to sketchnote!** Taking visual notes that make sense to you is what's important; your sketchnotes don't have to make sense to anyone else. I wrote this book to meet the needs of beginner sketchnoters by teaching the basic elements of sketchnoting and to help them build their visual vocabulary for use in sketchnotes.

2. Why sketchnote?

Sketchnoting offers so many benefits. Studies have proven that images are much more effective than words when it comes to memory retention, comprehension, and motivation (see index for relevant studies). There are psychological benefits as well because sketchnoting has a calming effect similar to that of meditation and listening to soothing music. Sketchnoting also allows students to see the bigger picture in the concepts they are studying, make connections in their learning, and display their learning process. Every teacher I have talked to who has introduced sketchnoting to their students has claimed that the practice has positively transformed the learning environment. Students love sketchnoting and are more engaged in class when using this method. Note-taking becomes more meaningful and fun when doodles are added to text. It quickly becomes a favourite activity for many learners.

Caleb Hoffmann was a student in grade ten when he began using sketchnoting as a way to take class notes. He says that it has been extremely helpful for him because he is a visual learner. You can watch his two-minute video at bit.ly/CalebHoffmann or scan the QR code shown here on a mobile device.

Adam Juarez (@techcoachjuarez) is an EdTech coach from California who has encouraged students at his school to sketchnote in all subject areas. To see the gallery of his students' sketchnotes, please visit: bit.ly/CardinalSketchnotes.

(For a colour version, visit bit.ly/WhySketchnote.)

3. How can you use sketchnotes in class?

There are many ways to use sketchnoting in class. When I taught French, I used it to introduce new vocabulary and as a form of storytelling.

Beth Matusciwitz (@MrsM_NL) is a kindergarten teacher who asks her students to doodle whenever she reads a story out loud. She says that her students are much more attentive to the story when they are doodling and that she is amazed at their level of engagement during this activity.

Jody Meacher (@meacherteacher) is a teacher who drew this sketchnote to describe other ideas to use sketchnoting in class:

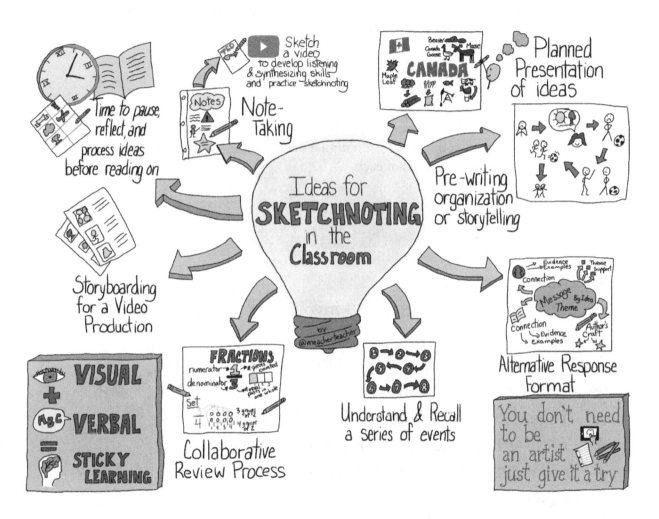

(For a colour version visit bit.ly/JodyMSketch.)

Many other teachers use sketchnotes in class in some pretty amazing ways. (I've included a list of sketchnoting educators and their resources and ideas at the end of this book.) Once you start sketchnoting with your students, you will discover all kinds of ways to integrate it in the classroom with every subject!

4. Analog or digital?

When you start sketchnoting yourself or with your students, you will need to determine if you want to use a digital device or pen/pencils/marker on paper. Let's look at the pros of each:

Analog Sketchnoting: The Pros

★ Less expensive
★ Easier to have whole class involved if you don't have a device for everyone
★ "Unplugged" option for non-screen time
★ Connection to childhood
★ Students can collaborate on a big drawing
★ Less tech to navigate for young children
★ Fewer distractions/temptations to wander off-task and g online

Digital sketchnoting: The Pros

★ All drawing tools within app
★ Lots of colours
★ Tablets are mobile
★ Easy to save work for later retrieval
★ Easy to share and archive images
★ "Undo" and eraser features
★ Different paint brushes for different effects
★ Different textures to draw on
★ Zooming in allows for finer detail in your drawings
★ Some apps allow for screencasting to record process
★ Some apps allow you to move items around canvas and resize
★ Ability to add grid which you can hide after
★ Layering
★ Tracing
★ Editing an existing sketchnote

5. Which apps and styluses should you draw with?

If you decide to try digital sketchnoting, there are many drawing apps to choose from. Karen Bosch (@karlyb) has a great resource page with many suggestions (bit.ly/KarenResources). My personal favourite drawing app is Procreate, which costs money but has many great features that make it a worthwhile purchase, such as layering, cutting and pasting, resizing objects, and exporting video. I have tried a number of the many styluses on the market and have concluded that my favourite is the Musemee Notier Prime because it has the finest point. If you have an iPad Pro, the Apple pencil is another excellent choice. Many sketchnoters don't use a stylus, preferring to draw with their finger.

 Pro Tip: Zoom in when you're drawing on the iPad to get to finer details in your sketchnotes.

6. How do you begin sketchnoting?

Most children under the age of ten love to draw. But for some reason, as we grow older, we tend to lose our love of drawing. Why is that? The answer varies from person to person, but during workshops when I ask this question, I most often hear that people lose their confidence with drawing, so they stop.

Before students can learn to sketchnote in class, the teacher needs to establish a doodling culture. Students need to know that it's okay to doodle in class, which may run counterintuitive to the way many teachers believe students pay attention. Many teachers (myself included—before I discovered the benefits of doodling) believe that a student needs to be looking directly at them to absorb the valuable information they are dispensing. Research, however, has proven the opposite: **Students are more likely to stay engaged in the lesson and to absorb and retain the information when they are doodling or sketchnoting** (see resource page for links to studies). Make pens, markers, and paper (or devices) available and easily accessible for students to use whenever they feel like doodling. Even better, give each student a notebook in which to keep their doodles and sketchnotes.

If you teach older students or adults, you may need to help them rediscover the fun and joy of drawing in addition to establishing a doodling culture. In the next chapter, you will find a number of scaffolded activities that you can do with your students of any age to relax them and to help them enjoy drawing. If you teach older students, begin by asking them to try to access their "inner child" and to recall a time when they loved to draw. After these scaffolded activities are completed, your students will be ready to learn about the more advanced elements and mechanics of sketchnoting (Chapters 3 and 4).

The important thing to stress in these activities—and in sketchnoting in general—is that there is no wrong or right way to sketchnote. It's a very personal process, and everyone's sketchnote will be unique.

 Learn more! For more tips and tricks for getting started with sketchnoting in the classroom, please take a look at this document with input from some of my edusketcher friends: bit.ly/TipsSketchnoters.

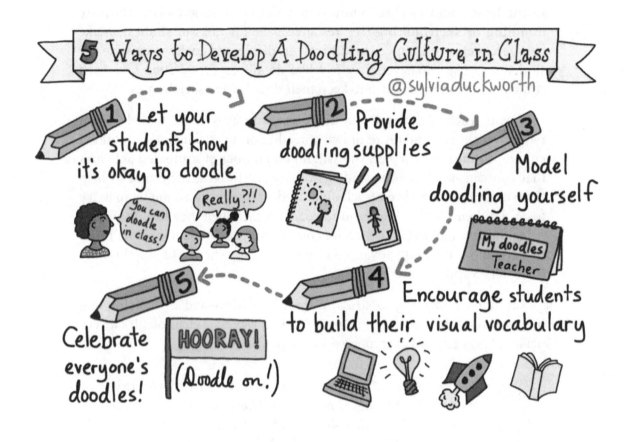

(To project this image in colour or to print it,
please visit bit.ly/5WaysDoodling)

Doodling Activities and Drawing Games

The best way to get your students ready for sketchnoting is to play some doodling and drawing games with them. These activities will get them in the mindset for sketchnoting. If you teach older students who have lost their love of drawing, these activities will also help bring the fun back into it.

I found two wonderful resources for drawing games: The first one is a book titled *Tangle Art and Drawing Games for Kids: A Silly Book for Creative and Visual Thinking* by Jeanette Nyberg (see resources). The second resource is the website ArtfulParent.com by Jean Van't Hul. Some of the activities below came from their resources.

I highly recommend that you play music to get those creative juices flowing while your students are drawing.

Doodling Challenge #1: Random Shapes

 Time to complete: 5 minutes

 Instructions: This is an individual activity. Give each student a piece of paper or digital device to draw on. Project the image below (bit.ly/RandomShape), or pre-draw the random shapes in a place where the students can see them. They are to choose one of the shapes and turn it into a doodle, getting as creative as possible. When they have finished one shape, they can try another shape, continuing this way until the music stops. Please add your own doodles to this challenge!

Doodling Challenge #2: Back-and-Forth Drawing

(from ArtfulParent.com)

 Time to complete: 5 minutes

 Instructions: This is a collaborative activity. With partners, all students have their own piece of paper or digital device to draw on. Students start off by drawing a random doodle or shape on their own piece of paper. They will then pass the paper to their partner, who will add to the drawing. This will continue going back and forth until the music ends. The teacher can tell students when to switch or leave it up to them to decide when to switch.

To view a video example, visit
bit.ly/BackForth, or scan the QR code.

Doodling Challenge #3: Interactive Heart Drawings

(from ArtfulParent.com)

 Time to complete: 5 minutes

 Instructions: This is a collaborative activity. With partners, all students have their own piece of paper or digital device to draw on. Each student will start off by drawing a little heart in the centre of the page, then pass the drawing to their partner, who will add a layer to it. Activity will continue this way until the drawing is complete.

 Variation: Let each student decide what shape they want to start the drawing with. Maybe a diamond, a square, or a random shape instead of a heart.

To view a video example, visit bit.ly/HeartDrawing, or scan the QR code.

Doodling Challenge #4: Icons with shapes

 Time to complete: 15 minutes

 Instructions: This is an individual activity. All students have their own piece of paper or digital device to draw on. Draw a circle and give the students one minute to create something with the circle (similar to doodling challenge #1). Then have them draw along with you the circle icons below. Repeat same instructions with a square, a triangle, and an oval.

Doodling Challenge #5: Mystery Doodles

 Time to complete: 5 minutes

 Instructions: This is an individual activity. All students have their own piece of paper or digital device to draw on. Draw these doodles in a large fashion, slowly, one by one, on the board or on a large piece of chart paper or on a reflected device where students can watch you. Students are to draw along with you. Do not tell them what you are drawing! If they think they know what you are drawing, they are to shout out loud what they think it is. Continue drawing until everyone has completed each doodle. Please add your own doodles to this challenge!

Visit bit.ly/MysteryIcons to view a video of how to draw these icons, or scan the QR code.

Doodling Challenge #6:
Words That Look like Their Meaning

 Time to complete: 5 minutes

 Instructions: This is an individual activity. All students have their own piece of paper or digital device to draw on. Project the image below (bit.ly/WordsMeaning) and explain that they will need to make some words look like their meaning as in the following examples:

Doodling Challenge: Draw the word "COLD" in a way that looks cold.

After they have finished, encourage your students to share their drawings. You can show them the drawing below as an example (bit.ly/ColdDoodle). Point out how the little curved lines around the letters help convey a shivering movement. Invite them to come up with their own words to draw.

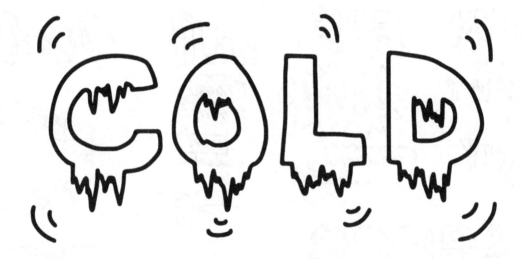

Doodling Challenge #7:
Letters That Look like Their Meaning

 Time to complete: 5 minutes

 Instructions: This is an individual activity. All students have their own piece of paper or digital device to draw on. Show the image below (bit.ly/GiffenSketch for a colour version) and explain that in this challenge they will need to make just some letters in the word to look like its meaning, as in the following examples:

Sketches by Jen Giffen @VirtualGiff

Doodling Challenge: Draw the word "HOT," choosing just one letter to look hot. If you finish one letter, try drawing another letter to look hot.

Afterward you can show your students the drawing below as an example (bit.ly/HotDoodle). Remind them that there is no right or wrong way to doodle and sketchnote.

Doodling Challenge #8: Fingerprint Doodles

 Time to complete: 5 minutes

 Instructions: This is an individual activity. All students have their own piece of paper to draw on and some washable markers. Show the image below (bit.ly/fingerprintanimals) and explain that in this challenge, they will make some fun fingerprint doodles.

Note: This idea is from the wonderful Ed Emberley book titled *Ed Emberley's Complete Funprint Drawing Book.*

Doodling Challenge #9: One-Minute Self-Portrait

 Time to complete: 1 minute

 Instructions: This is an individual activity. All students have their own piece of paper or digital device to draw on. If they have a digital device, ask them to take a selfie to look at while they draw a self-portrait (or have them look in a mirror). Ask them to quickly draw themselves, giving them no more than a minute to do it. You can show them the example below of my selfie (bit.ly/SylSelfie). Tell them to *keep it simple!*

Doodling Challenge #10:
One-Minute Portrait of Someone Else

 Time to complete: 1 minute

 Instructions: This is an individual activity. All students have their own piece of paper or digital device to draw on. If they have a digital device, ask them to take a picture of a friend in class to look at while they draw a portrait. (If there are no digital devices, they can take turns posing for each other.) Ask them to quickly draw their friend, giving them no more than a minute to do it. You can show them the example below of the portrait I drew of Albert Einstein (bit.ly/AlbertSketch). Remind your students to *keep it simple!*

 Variation: Ask your students to draw portraits of members of their family or of famous people.

Doodling Challenge #11: Pictionary™

 Time to complete: 10 minutes

 Instructions: This is a game to play in partners. All students have their own piece of paper or digital device to draw on. Ask one partner to draw and the other partner to guess what the doodle is. The guessers need to be turned away from the board. Project or write the first word on the board. Allow only fifteen seconds for the drawer and the guesser to guess the word. After fifteen seconds, show the word to the guesser, and ask students to share how they drew the word. Now ask partners to switch. Continue the game to the end.

You can use the words below or make up your own words. For a slide of these words, visit bit.ly/PictionarySketch.

1. Beard
2. Clown
3. Sofa
4. Breakfast
5. Sprinkler
6. Junk mail
7. Leprechaun
8. Puppeteer
9. Selfie
10. Video game

After you have finished the eleven doodling challenges above, your students should be warmed up and ready to sketchnote!

Chapter Three

Sketchnoting Icons and Building Your Visual Vocabulary

Sketchnoting icons are the bread and butter of sketchnoting. These little doodles, in combination with text, are what create a sketchnote. The cool thing about icons is that they can be used to represent many different things. Take a look at the icons below:

A computer can represent technology, research, connectivity, twenty-first-century skills, digital learning, etc. A light bulb can represent an idea, creativity, imagination, an *aha!* moment, etc. A rocket ship can represent the future, innovation, a voyage, an adventure, ignition, etc.

Sketchnoter Kate Hayward once said that you only need about one hundred sketchnoting icons to tell any story (TEDx Talk: bit.ly/HaywardTedTalk). The challenge for the beginner sketchnoter is building their own visual dictionary of sketchnoting icons. Over time and with experience sketchnoting, you will collect a vast repertoire of icons that you can use to represent many different things.

Pro Tip: Sketchnoter Carrie Baughcum (@HeckAwesome) has dedicated a board in her classroom for sketchnoting icons. She has sticky notes readily available so that when one of her students has an idea for an icon, he/she will draw it on the sticky note with its word and post it on the board.

Some abstract concepts are challenging to draw, and a representative icon can help make those concepts clear. Below are some ideas.

(For a larger image to project or print out, visit bit.ly/AbstractIcons.)

Icon Challenge

Project or show the icons below to your students. Discuss what each icon could represent. Remember that each icon can represent many different things.

(To project or print out image, visit: bit.ly/SylviaIcons.)

Doodling Challenge #12: Twenty-Second Icons

When sketchnoting, it is critical to remember not to spend a lot of time drawing icons. Sketchnotes are very fast doodles—don't strive for perfection. In the following challenge, show an icon to your students for only twenty seconds and have them draw them in a similar way—or in their own way. While they are drawing, read out loud the ideas for what these icons can represent. You can use this slide deck: bit.ly/TwentySecond.

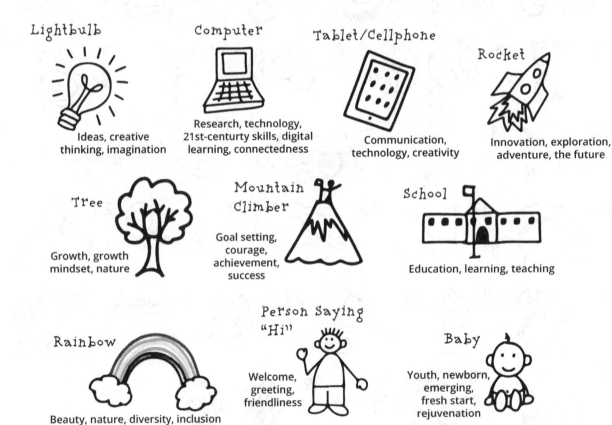

Lightbulb
Ideas, creative thinking, imagination

Computer
Research, technology, 21st-century skills, digital learning, connectedness

Tablet/Cellphone
Communication, technology, creativity

Rocket
Innovation, exploration, adventure, the future

Tree
Growth, growth mindset, nature

Mountain Climber
Goal setting, courage, achievement, success

School
Education, learning, teaching

Rainbow
Beauty, nature, diversity, inclusion

Person Saying "Hi"
Welcome, greeting, friendliness

Baby
Youth, newborn, emerging, fresh start, rejuvenation

Chapter Four

The Online Sketchnoting Icon Database

I have created an online digital database for sketchnoting icons so you can retrieve an icon in seconds if you are having a hard time coming up with an idea for one yourself. For access to the database, visit my site: sylviaduckworth.com > Sketchnote Course > Password = SDCourse. Please note that the database works best on a laptop.

How to Use the Database

The database is linked to four slide decks. On the same webpage, you will find direct links to the slide decks (I have split the slide decks into four because the pages would take too long to load in one slide deck). When looking for an icon in the spreadsheet, search for the concept you are trying to draw by holding the Cmd/Ctrl button down + F. A search cell will pop up in the top right-hand corner of the sheet. Type the term you are looking for (e.g., "Dilemma"). The word will be highlighted in green if it's in the database. Tap slightly above on the blue linked icon which will take you to the icon in the slide deck.

Of course, you *do not* need to use these icons in your sketchnotes. They are merely suggestions. Another good place to look for icons is TheNounProject.com, but these are not in sketchnote style.

If you do not have a laptop at your disposal, you can use the icons in Chapter 9 for ideas; however, they are not easily searchable.

I ask that you please do not share the Icon Database on any public forum.

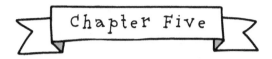

Chapter Five

Other Elements of Sketchnoting

Sketchnoting elements extend far beyond icons. Carol Anne McGuire (@rockourworld) has created this wonderful cheat sheet of the elements for sketchnoting, which she has posted online for a free download. You can print these out for your students when they begin sketchnoting:

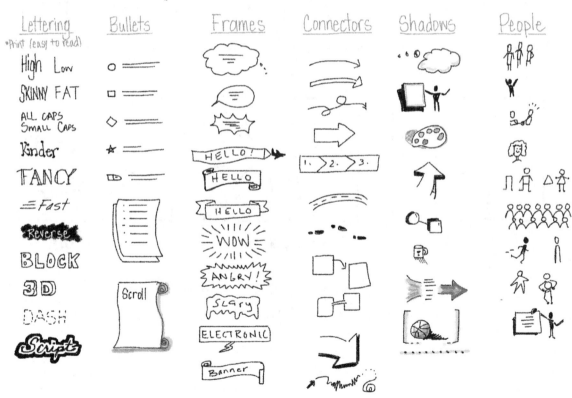

(You can access these tips at bit.ly/SketchnoteTips.)

1. Structures

You can decide ahead of time how you want to organize your sketchnote, or you can keep it more organic, just seeing where the drawing takes you. Over time you will likely develop your own style of structure for your sketchnotes.

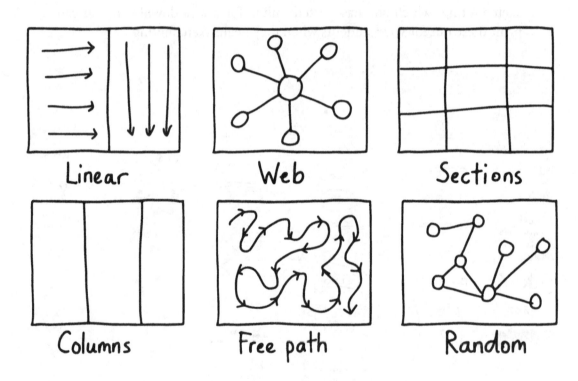

Linear   Web   Sections

Columns   Free path   Random

(To see this image in colour or to project it, visit bit.ly/SketchStructure.)

2. Fonts

Fonts are a lot of fun to practice, and over time you will select your favourites and will most likely create your own. I really only use about three to four different fonts for my sketchnotes, so you don't need a huge repertoire. Below are some examples. If you search Google or Pinterest for "Sketchnote fonts" you will find many more fonts to practice drawing.

Aa Bb Cc Dd Ee Ff Gg Hh Ii Jj Kk Ll Mm
Nn Oo Pp Qq Rr Ss Tt Uu Vv Ww Xx Yy Zz

Aa Bb Cc Dd Ee Ff Gg Hh Ii Jj Kk Ll Mm
Nn Oo Pp Qq Rr Ss Tt Uu Vv Ww Xx Yy Zz

Aa Bb Cc Dd Ee Ff Gg Hh Ii Jj Kk Ll Mm
Nn Oo Pp Qq Rr Ss Tt Uu Vv Ww Xx Yy Zz

ABCDEFGHIJKLM
NOPQRSTUVWXYZ

abcdefghijklm
nopqrstuvwxyz

ABCDEFGHIJKLM
NOPQRSTUVWXYZ

abcdefghijklmn
opqrst uvwxyz

ABCDEFGHIJKLMN
OPQRSTUVWXYZ

ABCDEFGHIJKLM
NOPQRSTUVWXYZ

ABCDEFGHIJKLMN
OPQRSTUVWXYZ

Aa Bb Cc Dd Ee Ff Gg Hh Ii
Jj Kk Ll Mm Nn Oo Pp Qq Rr
Ss Tt Uu Vv Ww Xx Yy Zz

ABCDEFGHIJKLMN
OPQRSTUVWXYZ

ABCDEFGHIJKLMN
OPQRSTUVWXYZ

abcdefghijklm
nopqrstuvwxyz

ABCDEFGHIJKLM
NOPQRSTUVWXYZ

abcdefghijklmn
opqrst uvwxyz
ABCDEFGHIJKLM
NOPQRSTUVWXYZ
ABCDEFGHIJKLM
NOPQRSTUVWXYZ

Aa Bb Cc Dd Ef Gg Hh Ii Jj Kk Ll Mm Nn Oo Pp Qq Rr Ss Tt Uu Vv Ww Xx Yy Zz

Aa Bb Cc Dd Ee Ff Gg Hh Ii Jj Kk Ll Mm Nn Oo Pp Qq Rr Ss Tt Uu Vv Ww Xx Yy Zz

ABCDEFGHIJKLM NOPQRSTUVWXYZ

ABCDEFGHIJKLMN
OPQRSTUVWXYZ
ABCDEFGHIJKLMN
OPQRSTUVWXYZ
ABCDEFGHIJKLMN
OPQRSTUVWXYZ

Numbers

0123456789 0123456789

0123456789

0123456789

0123456789 012

0123456789 345

0123456789 6789

(For the colour version of these fonts or to
project the images, visit bit.ly/FontsSyl.)

3. Banners

When drawing a banner, it is important to write the text first and then draw the banner around it. If you start with the banner, you may not be able to fit the text inside! Here are some examples of banners:

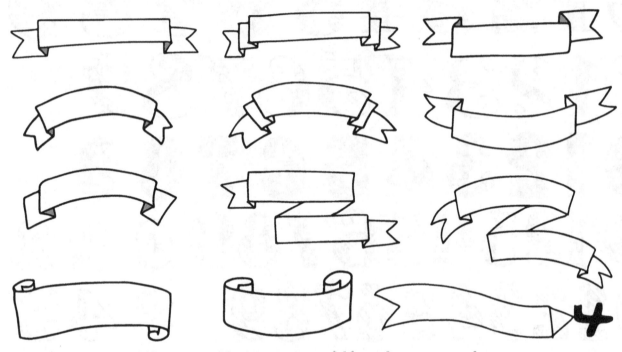

(To see a colour version of these banners or to project the image, visit bit.ly/ColorBanners.)

Please visit bit.ly/SDBanners for a video on how to draw banners or scan the QR code.

4. Containers/Frames

Containers or frames are used to draw attention or to isolate certain parts of your sketchnote. Here are some examples:

(To see a colour version of these containers and frames or to project the image, visit bit.ly/SketchFrames.)

Please visit bit.ly/SDContainers for a video on how to draw containers and frames or scan the QR code.

5. Arrows

Here are some different ways to draw arrows. Keep in mind that you do not need fancy arrows in a sketchnote. These are just some ideas if you want to embellish your sketchnote:

(To see a colour version of these arrows or to project the image, visit bit.ly/SketchArrows.)

Please visit bit.ly/SDArrows for a video on how to draw arrows or scan the QR code.

6. Bullets/Dividers

If you are creating a sketchnote with several points, consider using fancier bullet points for variety. Also, dividers are a way to compartmentalize different things in your sketchnote.

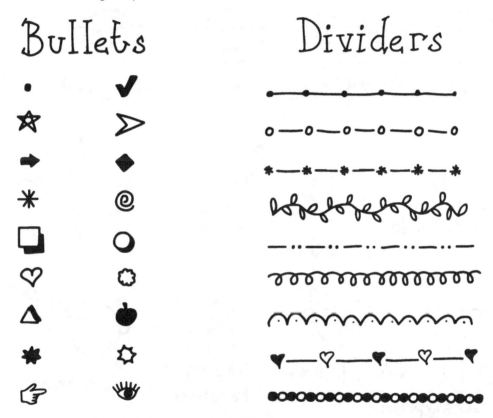

Bullets

Dividers

(To print or project the image, visit bit.ly/BulletsDividers.)

Please visit bit.ly/BulletsSD for a video on how to draw these icons or scan the QR code.

7. Faces

Drawing faces to convey emotion is very easy to do with just a few basic features.

Happy   Really happy   Sad   Really sad   Uncertain

Disgusted/Sick   Angry   Really angry   Confused   Scare

Shocked/surprised   Sleepy/bored   Frustrated   Laughing   Worrie

(To see a colour version of these faces or to project this image, visit bit.ly/SketchFaces.)

Please visit bit.ly/SDFaces for a video on how to draw arrows or scan the QR code

The faces on the previous page were drawn with these basic components (noses optional!):

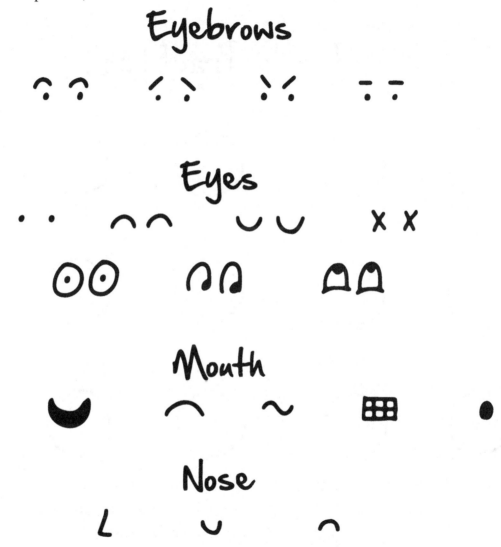

Eyebrows

Eyes

Mouth

Nose

(To project this image or to print out,
visit bit.ly/FaceComponents.)

Practice drawing faces by drawing circles and filling them with the different face components.

Let's Practice!

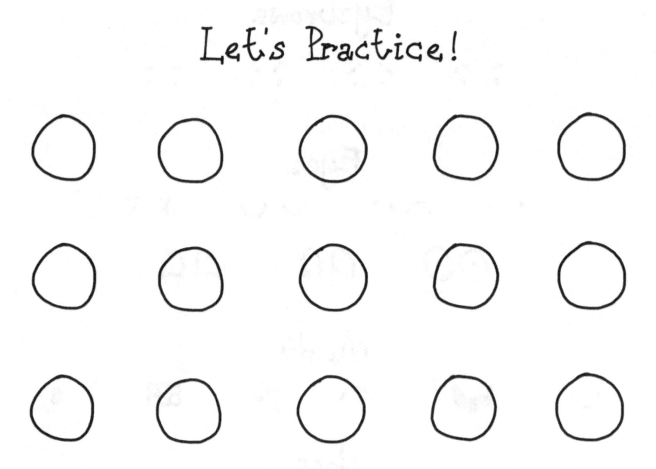

(To project this image or to print out, visit bit.ly/facecircles.)

Note: Emoticons are a great source for ideas on how to draw faces.

(For a colour version or to project,
visit bit.ly/EmoticonsExample.)

8. Hairstyles

Now let's draw some hair on top of the faces. Here are some examples of different hairstyles:

Long hairstyles

(To see a colour version of these hairstyles or to project, visit bit.ly/LongHairSyl.)

Please visit bit.ly/SylLongHair for a video on how to draw arrows or scan the QR code.

Short hairstyles

(To see a colour version of these hairstyles
or to print out and/or project,
visit bit.ly/ShortHairSyl.)

Please visit bit.ly/SylShortHair for a video
on how to draw arrows or scan the QR code.

9. Stick people

It doesn't take much to convey different actions with stick people. Here are some that you can practice drawing.

Conversation

Fighting Afraid

Motivated

Relaxed

Dancing

Sitting

Multi-tasking

Hugging

Sad Proud Shy Angry

Family

(To see a colour version of these stick people, visit bit.ly/StickPpl.)

Please visit bit.ly/SDPeople for a video on how to draw people or scan the QR code.

Over time, you will likely develop your own way to draw people. Here are few more ideas for drawing people:

(To see a colour version of these people or to project, visit bit.ly/SketchPeople.)

10. Transportation

Here are some transportation icons:

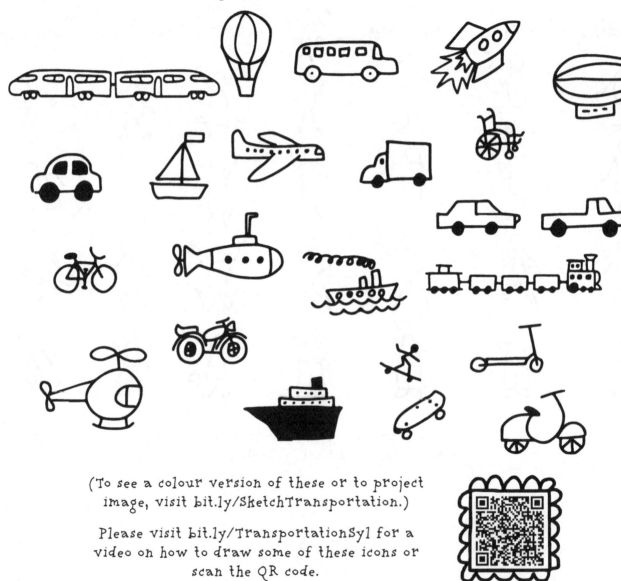

(To see a colour version of these or to project image, visit bit.ly/SketchTransportation.)

Please visit bit.ly/TransportationSyl for a video on how to draw some of these icons or scan the QR code.

11. Animals

Here are some animal icons:

(To see a colour version of these animals or to project image, visit bit.ly/SketchAnimals.)

Please visit bit.ly/AnimalsSyl for a video on how to draw some of these icons or scan the QR code.

12. Shading

Shading adds depth to your icons and can help them stand out. Try to imagine a bright light shining from one side, then add the shadow on the opposite side. There are two ways to do shading: shading on the outside edge of the icon or shading on the inside edge.

On the outside

On the inside

(To project or print out this image, visit bit.ly/ShadingSD.)

Live Sketchnoting

Live sketchnoting (doodling while someone is talking) is the most challenging form of sketchnoting. It is stressful at first, but it gets easier over time with practice. Here are some tips for live sketchnoting:

1. Before you begin, draw a banner, maybe a portrait of the speaker, the date and place. This will settle you down and get the creative juices flowing for sketchnoting.

2. You don't have to write down everything; just capture the parts that stick out for you. Capturing ten to twenty points of the talk is fine.

3. You can add more doodles/icons later.

4. You can add containers, colours, and other sketchnoting embellishments later.

5. *Don't stress!* Sketchnoting is supposed to be fun! Don't worry about the quality of your sketchnote; just get the key points down.

I enjoy live sketchnoting during keynote addresses in conferences. When I'm finished, I share my sketchnote as a gift with the speaker, who is always delighted to receive it. With the Procreate app that I draw with on my iPad, I can export the sketchnote as a video from the beginning to the end of my drawing. In iMovie, I can then add music and upload to YouTube. To see a YouTube playlist of my live sketchnotes, visit bit.ly/SylLiveSketchnotes.

(To project this image in colour or to print it,
please visit bit.ly/5TipsLive)

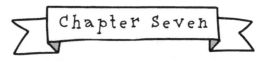

Chapter Seven

Let's Practice!

As with any other skill, if you want to get better at sketchnoting you will need to practice. I like to practice when I am watching TV (okay, when I'm listening to TV). It means I can binge-watch something and still feel like I'm being productive! For additional practice, you (and your students) can visit these websites for some daily doodling prompts: Sketch50.org and bit.ly/doodleadaychallenge.

Ideas to practice

Sketchnote...

1. A favourite quote
2. A blogpost
3. A joke
4. A card
5. A TED Talk
6. A story
7. A movie
8. During a staff meeting
9. How-to instructions
10. A live Keynote or presentation

(To see a colour version or to project or print this image, visit bit.ly/IdeasPractice.)

One good activity to try for your very first sketchnote is to make a mind map. For inspiration, please take a look at the many hand-drawn mind maps found on the website LearningFundamentals.com.au/resources.

Another great idea for a first sketchnote is to draw a Selfie Sketchnote. Ask your students to draw a sketch about themselves. You can model the activity after the image below and focus on "Things I love," or you may elect to keep the activity open-ended, allowing for students to express their individuality.

(To see a colour version or to project the image, please visit bit.ly/SketchnoteSelfie.)

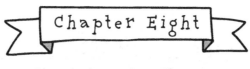

Chapter Eight

Sketchnote Fever

Working up to the launch of this book, I created a campaign to get the educational community excited about sketchnoting, called "#SketchnoteFever." Each lesson consists of a 3-minute video and an accompanying slide.

All of the lessons can be found on my website at bit.ly/sketchnotefever. For a complete slidedeck to project the images to your students, please visit bit.ly/31sketchnotefever.

(To project this image in colour or to print it,
please visit bit.ly/SketchnotefeverPoster)

Lesson 1: School Icons

Scan the QR code for Video

Lesson 1 #SketchnoteFever

Lesson 2: Easy Fonts

① Aa Bb Cc Dd Ee Ff Gg Hh Ii Jj Kk Ll Mm
Nn Oo Pp Qq Rr Ss Tt Uu Vv Ww Xx Yy Zz

② Aa Bb Cc Dd Ee Ff Gg Hh Ii Jj Kk Ll Mm
Nn Oo Pp Qq Rr Ss Tt Uu Vv Ww Xx Yy Zz

③ Aa Bb Cc Dd Ee Ff Gg Hh Ii Jj Kk Ll Mm
Nn Oo Pp Qq Rr Ss Tt Uu Vv Ww Xx Yy Zz

Scan the QR code for Video

Lesson 2 #SketchnoteFever

Lesson 3: Animal Icons

Scan the QR code for Video

Lesson 3 #SketchnoteFever

Lesson 4: Fancy Fonts

① ABCDEFGHIJKLM
NOPQRSTUVWXYZ

② ABCDEFGHIJKLM
NOPQRSTUVWXYZ
abcdefghijklm
nopqrstuvwxyz

Scan the QR code for Video

Lesson 4 #SketchnoteFever

Lesson 5: Transportation Icons

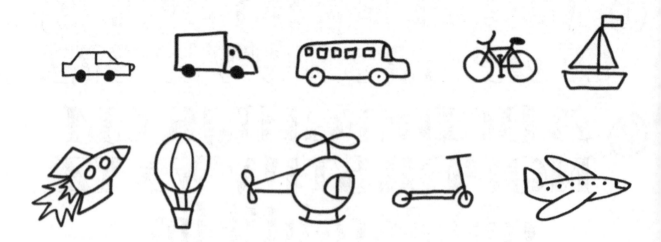

Scan the QR code for Video

Lesson 5 #SketchnoteFever

Lesson 6: More Fancy Fonts

③ ABCDEFGHIJKLMN
OPQRSTUVWXYZ

④ ABCDEFGHIJKLM
NOPQRSTUVWXYZ

Scan the QR code for Video

Lesson 6 #SketchnoteFever

Lesson 7: Weather Icons

Scan the QR code for Video

Lesson 7 #SketchnoteFever

Lesson 8: Food & Drink Icons

Scan the QR code for Video

Lesson 8 #SketchnoteFever

Lesson 9: Halloween Icons

Scan the QR code for Video

Lesson 9 #SketchnoteFever

Lesson 10: Banners

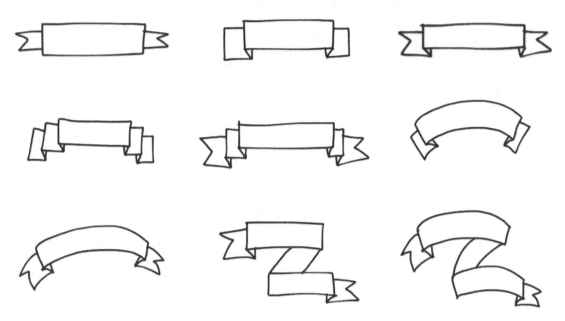

Scan the QR code for Video

Lesson 10 #SketchnoteFever

Lesson 11: Containers & Frames

Scan the QR code for Video

Lesson 11 #SketchnoteFever

Lesson 12: Arrows

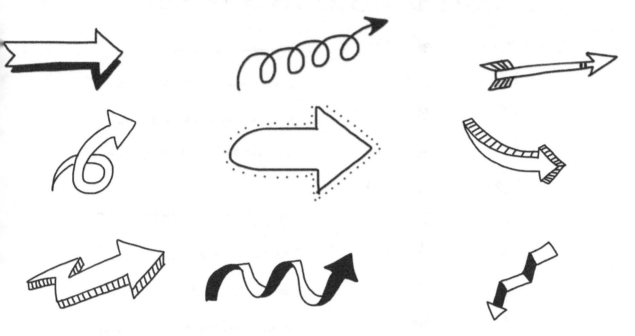

Scan the QR code for Video

Lesson 12 #SketchnoteFever

Lesson 13: Bullets & Dividers

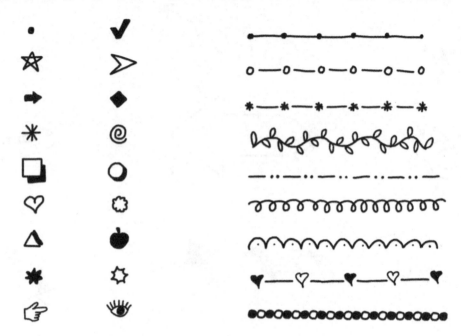

Scan the QR code for Video

Lesson 13 #SketchnoteFever

Lesson 14: Faces

Scan the QR code for Video

Lesson 14 #SketchnoteFever

Lesson 15: Female hairstyles

Scan the QR code for Video

Lesson 15 #SketchnoteFever

Lesson 16: Male hairstyles

Scan the QR code for Video

Lesson 16 #SketchnoteFever

Lesson 17: People

Scan the QR code for Video

Lesson 17 #SketchnoteFever

Lesson 18: School subjects

Scan the QR code for Video

Lesson 18 #SketchnoteFever

Lesson 19: More icons

Scan the QR code for Video

Lesson 19 #SketchnoteFever

Lesson 20a: Remembrance Day Icons

Scan the QR code for Video

Lesson 20a #SketchnoteFever

Lesson 20b: Even more icons

Scan the QR code for Video

Lesson 20b #SketchnoteFever

Lesson 21: Winter icons

Scan the QR code for Video

Lesson 21 #SketchnoteFever

Lesson 22: Spring things

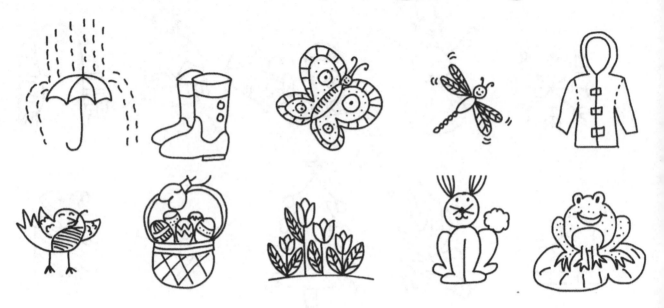

Scan the QR code for Video

Lesson 22 #SketchnoteFever

Lesson 23: Summer things

Scan the QR code for Video

Lesson 23 #SketchnoteFever

Lesson 24: Fall things

Scan the QR code for Video

Lesson 24 #SketchnoteFever

Lesson 25: Space things

Scan the QR code for Video

Lesson 25 #SketchnoteFever

Lesson 26: Sports

Scan the QR code for Video

Lesson 26 #SketchnoteFever

Lesson 27: Travelling icons

Scan the QR code for Video

Lesson 27 #SketchnoteFever

Lesson 28: Musical Instruments

Scan the QR code for Video

Lesson 28 #SketchnoteFever

Lesson 29: Hands

Scan the QR code for Video

Lesson 29 #SketchnoteFever

Lesson 30: Baby Things

Scan the QR code for Video

Lesson 30 #SketchnoteFever

Lesson 31: Wedding Things

Scan the QR code for Video

Lesson 31 #SketchnoteFever

Lesson 32: Social Media icons

Scan the QR code for Video

Lesson 32 #SketchnoteFever

Lesson 33: Table Things

Scan the QR code for Video

Lesson 33 #SketchnoteFever

Lesson 34: Kitchen Things

Scan the QR code for Video

Lesson 34 #SketchnoteFever

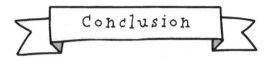

Conclusion

Now that you and your students have the basic tools for sketchnoting, it is my sincerest hope that sketchnoting will become a natural part of your daily routine. I can't wait to see what you create, and I would love to hear about your success stories. Please contact me at sduckworth100@gmail.com or through Twitter and Instagram at @sylviaduckworth to share your ideas or to ask any questions about sketchnoting.

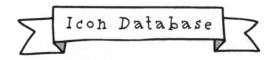

Icon Database

For easy access, here are all of the icons used in this book. Remember that you can access these digitally using the Online Icon Database. (See page 29 for instructions on accessing the Online Icon Database.)

1.
2.
3.
4.
5.
6.
7.
8.
9.
10.
11.
12.
13.
14.
15.
16.
17.
18.

19.

20.

21.

22.

23.

24. ? ?

25.

26.

27.

28.

29. LIST

30.

31.

32.

33.

34.

35.

36.

37.

38.

39. SCENE 1

40.

41.

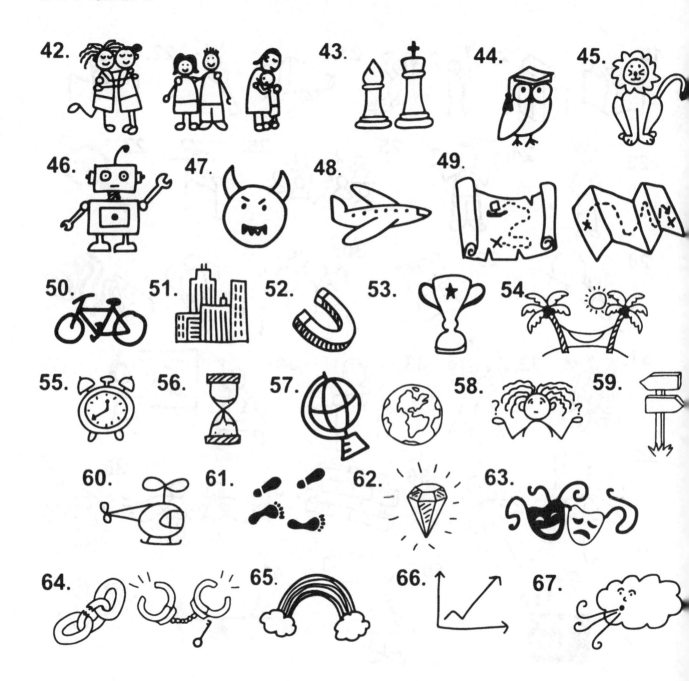

42. 43. 44. 45.
46. 47. 48. 49.
50. 51. 52. 53. 54.
55. 56. 57. 58. 59.
60. 61. 62. 63.
64. 65. 66. 67.

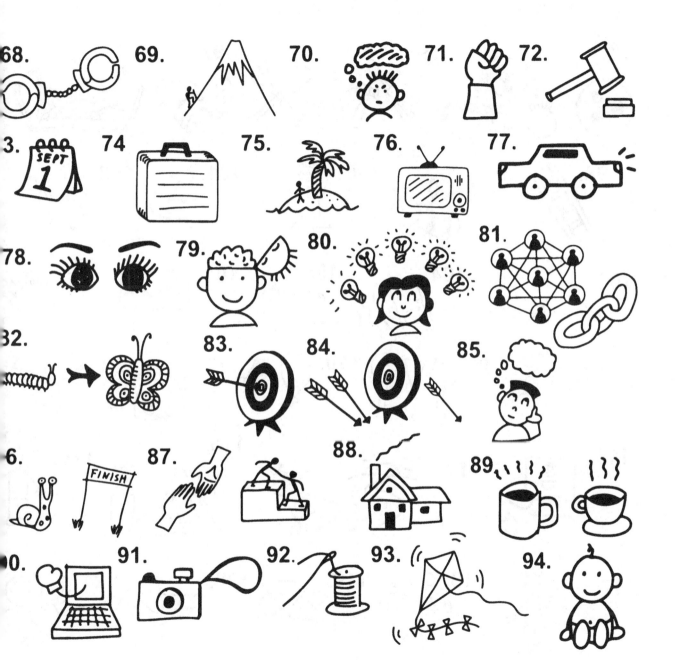

68.
69.
70.
71.
72.
3.
74.
75.
76.
77.
78.
79.
80.
81.
32.
83.
84.
85.
6.
87.
88.
89.
0.
91.
92.
93.
94.

FINISH
SEPT 1

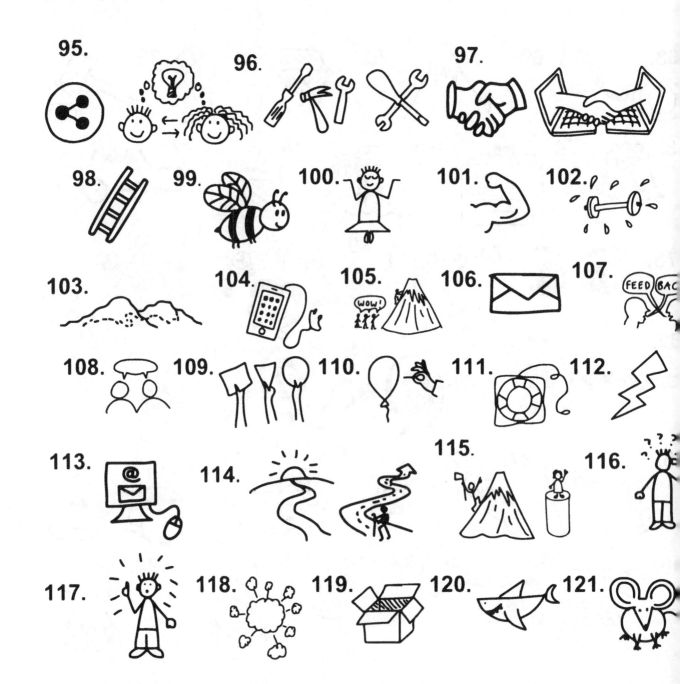

122. 123. 124. 125.
126. 127. 128. 129. 130.
131. 132. 133. 134.
135. 136. 137. 138. 139.
140. 141. 142. 143.
144. 145. 146.

147.

148.

149.

150.

151.

152.

153.

154.

155.

156.

157.

158.

159.

160.

161.

162.

163.

164.

165.

166.

167.

168.

169.

170.

171.

172.

173

174.

175.

176.

177.

178.

179.

180.

181.

182.

183.

184.

185.

186.

187.

188.

189.

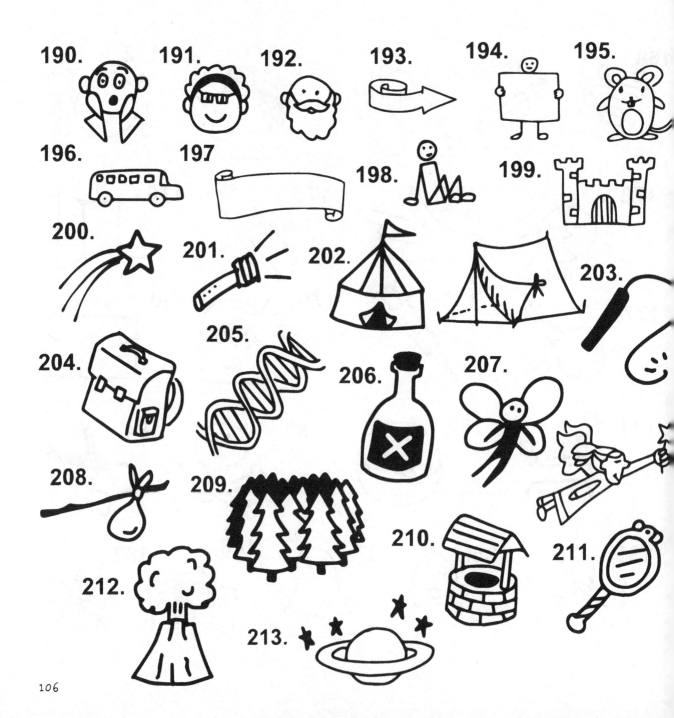

190.
191.
192.
193.
194.
195.
196.
197
198.
199.
200.
201.
202.
203.
204.
205.
206.
207.
208.
209.
210.
211.
212.
213.

214.

215.

216.

217.

218.

219.

220.

221.

222.

223.

224.

225.

226.

227.

228.

229.

230.

231.

232.

233.

234.

	Icon	To Represent
1	Lightbulb	Ideas, innovation, creative thinking
2	Computer	Technology, twenty-first-century skills, digital learning
3	iPad	Technology, creativity, tablet, digital
4	School	Education, learning, teaching
5	Tree	Growth, growth mindset, nature, life, family, stability, thrive
6	Mountain Climber #1	Goal setting, courage, achievement, success
7	Rocket	Innovation, exploring, excitement, adventure, the future, moon shot
8	Rainbow	Beauty, nature, serenity, diversity, inclusion
9	Person	Hello, waving, hi, friendly, welcome, welcoming, greet, greeting
10	Cat	Cute, feline, wily, animal
11	Dog	Cute, loyal, animal, eager
12	Birds	Freedom, nature, flying
13	School Bus	Education, school, travel, road trip, field trip
14	Fish and Diver	Explore, exploration, digging deeper, adventure, the ocean, nature
15	Pigs	Farm, animals, hog, cute, gluttony, bacon
16	Family	Love, togetherness, community, support, mother, father, sister, brother
17	Human Pyramid	Collaboration, collaborate, teamwork, friends, networking, trust
18	Brain	Intelligence, thinking, mindset
19	Books	Learning, education, intelligent
20	Joy	Happy, happiness, glee
21	Megaphone and Microphone	Voice, advocate, announce, announcement
22	Tightrope Walker	Risk taking, courage, stepping out of comfort zone
23	Holding up	Support, backup
24	Palms up	Choice, confusion, indecision
25	Crowd	People, students, group, audience
26	Hurdle	Overcoming obstacles, jumping, barriers
27	Magnifying Glass	Curious, curiosity, examine, focus, explore

	Icon	To Represent
28	Pushing Ball up Hill	Perseverance, dedication, tenacity, determination, grit
29	List	Things to do, busy, chores, tasks, responsible, responsibility
30	Balloons and Streamers	Party, celebration, celebrate, joy, festive, festivities
31	Fire	Passion, heat, purpose, ignite
32	Ribbon	Success, congratulations, self-esteem, goal setting, achievement, pride, proud
33	Podium	Leader, leadership, speaker, speaking, presenting, presentation, keynote, speech
34	Student and Teacher	Education, teaching, learning, class, classroom
35	Umbrella	Protect, protection, rain, hot weather, sunny
36	Brick wall	Fixed mindset, obstacle, barrier, stubborn, build, building, foundation
37	Superheroes	Courage, greatness, bravery
38	Paint Palette	Creativity, self-expression, art
39	Film Clapper	Film, video making, movies, creativity
40	Protester	Advocate, student voice, protest, disagree
41	Balance	Fairness, balanced life, equality
42	Hug	Kindness, friend, friendship, love, family, empathy, compassion
43	Chess Piece	Strategy, problem solving, planning
44	Owl	Wise, wisdom, sage, intelligent, intelligence
45	Lion	Bravery, courage, strength
46	Robot	Coding, robotics, futuristic, future
47	Devil	Evil, bad, wicked, dishonest
48	Airplane	Journey, adventure, travel, flight
49	Maps	Plan, journey, adventure, travel
50	Bicycle	Exercise, travel, transportation, urban
51	Buildings	City, urban, dwellings, apartments
52	Magnet	Attract, force, strong
53	Trophy	Success, winner, victory

	Icon	To Represent
54	Hammock	Relaxation, de-stressing, tropical, vacation
55	Clock	Time, stress, pressure, promptness, late
56	Hourglass	Time passing, pressure, time running out, stress, deadline
57	Globe, Earth	Environment, community, global
58	Choice	Dilemma, right or wrong, good or bad, problem
59	Signpost	Choice, right way wrong way, direction
60	Helicopter	Travel, parents, adventure
61	Footprints	Travel, wandering, digital, walking, following
62	Diamond	Precious, jewel, valuable
63	Masks	Drama, roles, happy/sad
64	Freedom	Freedom, liberty, broken shackles
65	Rainbow	Inclusion, diversity, beauty, nature, good luck, serenity
66	Graph	Improvement, growth, success, upward mobility
67	Wind	Windy, blowing, cold
68	Handcuffs	Restrained, oppression, trapped
69	Steep Mountain	Challenge, hard work, persistence, dedication, daunting
70	Dark Cloud	Doubt, anger, depression, anxiety
71	Fist	Solidarity, power, strong
72	Judge's Gavel	Justice, respect, honour, honesty, fairness
73	Calendar	Time, days, weeks, year
74	Suitcase	Travel, business, adventure
75	Island	Isolated, isolation, alone, stranded
76	TV	Entertainment, commercials, movies, media
77	Car	Trip, adventure, journey
78	Eyes	See, watch, scrutinize, observe
79	Open-Minded	Open-minded, flexibility, openness
80	Ideas/Brainstorming	Ideas, brainstorming, imagination

	Icon	To Represent
81	Links	Network, connectedness, PLN, connections
82	Caterpillar to Butterfly	Transform, transformation, change, growth
83	Bulls-Eye	Goal, success, achievement
84	Missed Bulls-Eye	Failure, perseverance, trying
85	Thinking	Reflection, thoughts, contemplation
86	Snail Finish	Slow, steady, persistence
87	Helping Hands	Help, support, reaching
88	House	Home, safe, comfort
89	Coffee and Tea	Relaxing, comfort, coffee break
90	Online Bullying	Mean, digital citizenship, ganging up
91	Camera	Travel, adventure, documenting
92	Needle and Thread	Fix, repair, mend
93	Kite	Play, carefree, childhood
94	Baby	Youth, beginning, birth, rejuvenation
95	Share	Sharing, social media, collaborating
96	Tools	Ability, industrious, critical thinking
97	Handshake	Respect, honour, dignity, friendship, compassion, digital citizenship, integrity
98	Ladder	Climbing, upward mobility, step up, scaffolding
99	Bee	Busy, industrious, hardworking
100	Yoga	Well-being, calmness, balance
101	Strong Arm	Strength, muscle, workout
102	Dumb Bells	Strength, workout, hard work
103	Mountain Trip	Travel, voyage, trip, hike
104	Mobile Phone	Technology, communication, creativity, music
105	Mountain Climber #2	Admire, admiration, role model, hard work, perseverance
106	Envelope	Communication, mail, correspondence

	Icon	To Represent
107	Feedback	Collaboration, honestly, colleagues
108	Conversation	Talk, chat, collaboration
109	Different	Diversity, inclusion, differentiation
110	Disruption	Status-quo change, challenge, flip
111	Lifesaver	Saviour, help, support
112	Lightning Bolt	Power, powerful, *coup de foudre*, flash, electricity, shocking
113	Email	Communication, digital correspondence, inbox
114	Road	Future, sunrise, opportunity, travel, adventure, hiking
115	Leadership	Leader, role model, mentor
116	Questions	Confused, wondering, undecided
117	Understand	Realize, realization, comprehension
118	Explosion	Disruption, fighting, argument
119	Box	Thinking outside the box, boxed in, escape
120	Shark	Danger, ocean, fish, assertive, aggression
121	Mouse	Mousey, small, tiny, rodent, critter, timid, cute
122	Elephant	Huge, large, enormous, gigantic, memory
123	Forest	Woods, nature, outdoors, environment
124	Spotlight	Perform, performance, stage, star
125	Telescope	Explore, exploration, curious, discovery, adventure
126	Tombstone	Death, finality, demise
127	Music notes	Musical, harmony, singing
128	Shrugging Shoulders	Uncertain, indecision, I don't know, choice
129	Lock and Key	Open, restriction, freedom, secure, private
130	Positive Attitude	Optimist, optimism, bright future, happy
131	Gears	Problem solving, solution, critical thinking
132	Magic Wand	Special, wizard, wizardry
133	Low Battery	Tired, fatigue, out of juice, exhausted

	Icon	To Represent
134	Dreamer	Dreams, dreaming, imagination
135	Crossed Arms	Stubborn, determined, strong minded, no
136	Patience	Good, saintly, sweet
137	Money Bag	Rich, wealthy, money, finances, financial
138	Puzzle Pieces	Problem solving, solution, critical thinking
139	Binoculars	Looking closer, examination, view, watch
140	Dove	Peace, unity, harmony
141	Scales	Justice, rights, fairness, balance
142	Science Beakers	Experimenting, trying out, project
143	Bridge	Trust, troubled waters, friendship
144	Juggling	Multitasking, stress, busy, practice
145	Dice	Random, dicey, chance, risky
146	Heart in Hands	Passion, compassion, trust, sincerity
147	Wow!	Amazing, amazement, accomplishment
148	Safety Net	Safe, secure, support
149	Conference	Face-to-face, meeting, professional development
150	Hang Glider	Freedom, innovation, iteration, flying
151	Scribble	Messy, disorder
152	Confused Face	Complicated, uncertain
153	Prayer	Sincere, sincerity, religion, hope
154	Pride/Proud	Accomplishment, self-worth
155	Sad	Sadness, depression, disappointment
156	Victory	Win, winning, achievement
157	Finger with String	Remember, don't forget, Important
158	ABC	Learn, learning, school, education
159	Book + Magnifying Glass	Research, investigate
160	Exclamation Mark	Important

	Icon	To Represent
161	People at Table	Meeting, group
162	Weights	Strong, strength, exercise
163	Boy and Girl	Friends, friendship, sister and brother
164	Thumbs-up	Positive, positivity, good, competent, competence, ok, okay
165	Beaver	Busy, industrious, hardworking, productivity, productive
166	Lighthouse	Guide, guidance, guiding, lead, leading, leadership
167	Notebook	School, note-taking, writing, notes
168	Pencil	Note-taking, writing, write, notes
169	Pen	Writing, write, scribble
170	Ear	Listen, listening, hear, hearing, paying attention
171	Talking	Talk, speak, speaking
172	Plate, Fork, Spoon, Knife	Food, eating, meals
173	Sun/Moon	Daytime, nighttime, contrast, opposite
174	Pointing Hand	Important, notice, this, look
175	Ruler	Rule, measure, distance
176	Door	Opportunity, open-door policy, escape
177	Bomb	Danger, time-ticking, terrorism
178	Needle	Illness, sickness, cure, medicine, doctor
179	Treasure Chest	Find, surprise, gift, reward, value, valuable, talent, ability, riches
180	Briefcase	Work, job, employment
181	Shopping Cart	Buying, consumer, sales, commerce
182	Compass	Navigate, orientation, leadership, direction, course
183	Skull and Bones	Death, danger, poison, risk, threat
184	Scissors	Cut, sever, snip
185	Cloud	Windy, hot air, blowing
186	Pizza	Delicious, snack, fast food
187	Ghost	Halloween, spooky, scary

	Icon	To Represent
188	Book with temple	History, civilization, school
189	Snowflake	Winter, snow, frosty, cold
190	Face	Surprised, shocked, overwhelmed
191	Glasses	Smart, intelligent, wise
192	Beard	Old, elderly, wise
193	Arrow	Direction, moving, change
194	Sign	Important, notice, announcement
195	Mouse	Cute, clever, quiet
196	Bus	Transportation, school, field trip
197	Scrolled banner	Important, notice, announcement
198	Sitting down	Relaxing, resting, student
199	Castle	Royalty, majestic, fairy tale, magic
200	Shooting star	Magic, celestial, imagination, astronomy
201	Flashlight	Searching, research, light
202	Tent	Circus, camping, outdoors, nature
203	Firecracker	Ignite, explosive, loud, celebration
204	Backpack, knapsack	Travel, school, student, homework
205	DNA	Double helix, genetics, hereditary, science, genes
206	Medicine	Illness, cure, sick, remedy, medical
207	Fairy	Imagination, story, fairytale, magic
208	Bag on stick	Homeless, wanderlust, travelling, wandering, adventuresome
209	Trees	Forest, nature, woods
210	Well	Water, dry, hole, hollow, wishing, hopeful
211	Mirror	Reflection, introspection, vanity, vain
212	Volcano	Explosion, Explosive, volatile, unpredictable, violent, blast
213	Planet	Space, exploration, astronomy, solar system
214	Bandaid/bandage	Remedy, fix, repair

	Icon	To Represent
215	First aid kit	Help, remedy, fix, health, emergency, safety
216	Creativity	Creative, artistic, imagination
217	Rollercoaster	Emotional, fair, joyride, adventurous, risky
218	Ballerina	Dance, arts, carefree, joy
219	Forget-me-not	Flower, remember, nature
220	Orchid	love, luxury, beauty, strength
221	Scientist	Science, profession, job, girlpower
222	Birthday cake	Celebration, childhood, candles
223	Mystery man	Mysterious, question, inigma, intrigue
224	Raincoat	Spring, rainy, protection
225	Pool	Summer, refreshing, cool down
226	Leaves	Fall, autumn, nature
227	Winner	Winning, race, success
228	Astronaut	Space, exploration, adventure
229	Statue of Liberty	Freedom, liberty, U.S.A., America
230	Piano	Jazz, music, creativity
231	Okay sign	Correct, good, right
232	Instagram	Selfie, social media, documentation
233	Bride and groom	Marriage, loyalty, family
234	Baby carriage	Newborn, rebirth, family

More Resources

Articles/Blogposts

Making Learning Visual Helps Memories Stick (bit.ly/MindShiftDoodling)

The Power of Visual Notetaking (bit.ly/PowerVisuals)

In Defense of Doodling (bit.ly/DoodlingDefense)

10 Creative Ways to Use Sketchnotes in the Classroom (bit.ly/10CreativeWaysSketch)

Memorisation Method Matters (bit.ly/MemorisationMethods)

The Benefits of Using Doodling and Sketchnotes in the Classroom (bit.ly/DoodlingBenefits)

Visual Note-taking: Keep focus and Improve Retention (bit.ly/VisualKeepFocus)

Dual Coding Theory and Visual Note-taking (bit.ly/DualCodingVisual)

The Powerful Science Behind Visual Note-taking (bit.ly/PowerfulVisuals

Sketchnoting the Path to Better Note-taking (bit.ly/SketchnotingPath)

Dual Coding and Common Coding Theories of Memory (bit.ly/DualCoding)

How Visual Notes Helped a Student With a Learning Disability Thrive (bit.ly/VisualNotesDis)

Drawing Is the Fastest, Most Effective Way to Learn (bit.ly/Drawing2Learn)

The Power of Visual Notetaking (bit.ly/Scriberia)

The Science of Drawing and Memory (bit.ly/DrawingScience)

Dual Coding Theory for Educators (bit.ly/DualCodingEdu)

Studies

What Does Doodling Do? By Jackie Andrade, in Applied Cognitive Psychology (bit.ly/WhatDoesDoodling)

Memorisation Methods in Science Education: Tactics to Improve the Teaching and Learning Practice (bit.ly/MemorisationMethods)

The Pen is Mightier than the Keyboard (bit.ly/MightyPen)

The Drawing Effect: Evidence for Reliable and Robust Memory Benefits in Free Recall (bit.ly/DrawingEffect)

The Surprisingly Powerful Influence of Drawing on Memory (bit.ly/DrawingMemory)

Books

Tangle Art and Drawing Games for Kids: A Silly Book for Creative and Visual Thinking by Jeanette Nyberg

Visual Vocab by Donna McGeorge

The Sketchnote Handbook by Mike Rohde

The Doodle Revolution by Sunni Brown

Any of Ed Emberley's *How-to-Draw* books

Visual Note-Taking for Educators by Wendi Pillars

Sketchnoting in School by Karin Perry, Holly Weimar, and Mary Ann Bell

21 Doodle Days by Diane Bleck

Discovery Doodles by Alicia Diane Durand (Diane Bleck)

Ink and Ideas: Sketchnotes for Engagement, Comprehension, and Thinking by Tanny McGregor

Online Resources

Sketch50.org

bit.ly/doodleadaychallenge

Artfulparent.com

SketchnoteArmy.com

ArtForKidsHub.com/how-to-draw

schrockguide.net/sketchnoting (Kathy Schrock)

YouTube Playlists

Carrie Baughcum (bit.ly/CarrieYTsketchnotes)

Sylvia Duckworth (bit.ly/SylYTsketchnotes)

How to Draw (bit.ly/YTHowToDraw)

Doodle Word Art (bit.ly/YTDoodleWordArt)

Karen Bosch (bit.ly/YTKarenBosch)

Doug Neill (bit.ly/SketchnoteSchool)
Diane Bleck (bit.ly/YTDianeBleck)
The Revision Guide (bit.ly/YTRevisionGuide)
Doodles by Sarah (bit.ly/SarahDoodles)

EduSketchnoters + Resources

Karen Bosch (@karlyb, bit.ly/KarenResources)
Silvia Tolisano (@langwitches, langwitches.org)
Carrie Baughcum (@heckawesome, carriebaughcum.com)
Royan Lee (@royanlee, bit.ly/RoyanLeeSketchnotes)
Jen Giffen (@virtualgiff, virtualgiff.com)
Wanda Terral (@wterral, ignitionedu.com)
Cate Tolnai (@catetolnai, catetolnai.com)
Marie-Andrée Ouimet (@maotechno, maotechno.com/sketchnotes)
Beth Matusciwitz (@MrsM_NL)
Carol Ann McGuire (@rockourworld, rockourworld.org)
Misty Kluesner (@MistyKluesner, bit.ly/MistyKluesner)
Larissa Aradj (@MrsGeekChic, MrsGeekChic.com)
Amanda Taylor (@TeacherAndGeek)
Ann Kozma (@AnnKozma723, techtravelteach.com)
Matt Miller (@jmattmiller, DitchThatTextbook.com)
Michele Osinski (@CheleOh, Techfairies.com)
Rabbi Michael Cohen (@TheTechRabbi, TheTechRabbi.com)
Nichole Carter (@MrsCarterHLA, bsdfutureready.com)
Stacy Duval (@staceyduval5, bit.ly/StaceyDuval)
Valeria Rodriguez (@valeriasketches, valeriasketches.com)
Rachel Swanson (@racheldswanson, SketchnoteWithRachel.blogspot.com)
Dana Ladenburger (@dladenburger)
Tanny McGregor (@tannyMcG, tannymcgregor.com)
Manuel S. Herrera (@manuelherrera33, instagram.com/manuelherrera33)
Giulia Forsythe (@giuliaforsythe, edudoodle.com)
Lorraine Kasyan (@lorrainekasyan, lorrainekasyan.com
Karin Perry (@kperry, karinlibrarian.booklikes.com

Holly Weimar (@drweimar)
Paola (@paola_edu, enseigneravecdesapps.com)
Rayna Freedman (@rlfreedm, msfreedmanagent24.blogspot.com)
Adam Juarez (@techcoachjuarez, sites.google.com/cojusd.org/
ohssketchnotesgallery/home)
Debby Penny (@DebbyPenny)

Other Notable Sketchnoters

Mike Rohde (@rohdesign, RohDesign.com)
Sunni Brown (@sunnibrown, SunniBrown.com)
Diane Bleck (@dianebleck, DoodleInstitute.mykajabi.com)
Doug Neil (@douglaspneill, VerbaltoVisual.com)

Twitter Hashtags

#sketch50
#doodleaday
#todaysdoodle
#doodle2learn
#IdeaFlood

#SketchCue
#SNHangout
#SketchnoteArmy
#SKETCHNOTEFEVER
#everyonecansketch

Instagram

@Diane.Bleck
@TheDoodleGuide
@sketch_50
@sninschool

@taraleighjohnston
@nataliaoro
@marijketekent
@bydawnnicole

Instagram hashtags

#sketchnoting
#sketch50
#sketchnotes
#sketchnotearmy
#doodles
#visualthinking

#education
#edudoodles
#infodoodles
#sketch2learn
#doodle2learn
#everyonecansketch

More Books from

ELEVATE BOOKS EDU

elevatebooksedu.com

Sketchnotes for Educators
100 Inspiring Illustrations for Lifelong Learners

By Sylvia Duckworth

Sylvia Duckworth is a Canadian teacher whose sketchnotes have taken social media by storm. Her drawings provide clarity and provoke dialogue on many topics related to education. This book contains 100 of her most popular sketchnotes with links to the original downloads that can be used in class or shared with colleagues. Interspersed throughout the book are Sylvia's reflections on each drawing and what motivated her to create them, in addition to commentary from other educators who inspired the sketchnotes.

The Google Infused Classroom
A Guidebook to Making Thinking Visible and Amplifying Student Voice

By Holly Clark and Tanya Avrith

This beautifully designed book offers guidance on using technology to design instruction that allows students to show their thinking, demonstrate their learning, and share their work (and voices!) with authentic audiences. *The Google Infused Classroom* will equip you to empower your students to use technology in meaningful ways that prepare them for the future.

Dive into Inquiry
Amplify Learning and Empower Student Voice

By Trevor MacKenzie

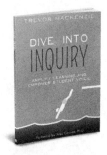

Dive into Inquiry beautifully marries the voice and choice of inquiry with the structure and support required to optimize learning. With *Dive into Inquiry* you'll gain an understanding of how to best support your learners as they shift from a traditional learning model into the inquiry classroom where student agency is fostered and celebrated each and every day.

Inquiry Mindset
Nurturing the Dreams, Wonders, and Curiosities of Our Youngest Learners

By Trevor MacKenzie and Rebecca Bathurst-Hunt

Inquiry Mindset offers a highly accessible journey through inquiry in the younger years. Learn how to empower your students, increase engagement, and accelerate learning by harnessing the power of curiosity. With practical examples and a step-by-step guide to inquiry, Trevor MacKenzie and Rebecca Bathurst-Hunt make inquiry-based learning simple.

Book Sylvia Duckworth to Speak at Your next Teacher Professional Development Session or Conference!

Sylvia is an award-winning teacher from Toronto, Canada, with 32 years classroom experience. She is a Google Certified Innovator and Trainer, Apple Distinguished Educator, and author of the books "Sketchnotes for Educators" and "How to Sketchnote: A Step-by-Step Manual for Teachers and Students".

Workshop Description:

Sketchnoting, or visual note-taking, is gaining widespread popularity as an effective and engaging way to take notes and to facilitate understanding and learning. Workshop participants will learn how to develop a doodling mentality with various fun and scaffolded drawing activities throughout the day. Sylvia will walk you through the basic elements of sketchnoting such as how to set up your sketchnote and how to draw icons, fonts, arrows, people, faces, animals, banners, containers, frames, bullets, dividers, and shading. By the end of the workshop, even the most reluctant artist will become a budding sketchnoter, and will leave with all the skills necessary to create beautiful and meaningful visual notes. Come and discover the magic of sketchnoting!

For more information or to book a workshop, please see . . .

SylviaDuckworth.com

 sduckworth100@gmail.com

@sylviaduckworth
(Twitter and Instagram)

Sylvia Duckworth is an award-winning teacher, Google Certified Innovator, and Apple Distinguished Educator who lives in Toronto, Canada, with her husband Steve and daughters Alana and Lauren. When she is not cycling the Toronto bicycle paths, Sylvia enjoys travelling around the world to teach people how easy it is to sketchnote. She blogs and shares her resources at sylviaduckworth.com and has an online store at sylviaduckworth.shop.

Made in the USA
Las Vegas, NV
01 January 2024

83773176R00077